JUNIOR NATURE GUIDE
BUTTERFLIES

Written by Susan McKeever

www.alligatorbooks.co.uk

Butterfly Hunter's Code

1 Always go collecting with a friend, and always tell an adult where you are going.
2 Treat all butterflies with care – they are delicate creatures and can be easily killed if roughly handled.
3 Ask permission before exploring or crossing private property.
4 Keep to footpaths as much as possible.
5 Keep off crops and leave fence gates as you find them.
6 Ask your parents not to light fires except in fire places in special picnic areas.
7 Take your litter home.

© 2006 Alligator Books Limited
Published by Alligator Books Limited
Gadd House, Arcadia Avenue,
London N3 2JU

Printed in Malaysia

Contents

What Is a Butterfly?

Fluttering butterflies live everywhere in Europe. You can spot them in a huge variety of places – on mountains, in damp bogs, in sunny woodlands, flying through meadows, and in your own back garden. You already know that they are beautiful to look at, but they also have a fascinating lifestyle.

This book will help you to become a butterfly spotter in two ways. It only shows you the butterflies that you are most likely to see, and it puts them in the habitat, or type of countryside, where you are most likely to see them.

Where butterflies choose to live depends a lot on the flowers and plants they like to feed on. So knowing a butterfly's favourite plant, and where it grows, is a great help toward knowing where to spot that butterfly.

The life of a butterfly

Butterflies go through four very different stages in their lives, and you can look for them at each stage. The first stage is the egg. Next comes the caterpillar, the chrysalis, and finally the butterfly.

Changing from one form to another like this is called complete metamorphosis (change in form) because the larval (young) stages are completely different from the adult.

The caterpillar hatches (it eats its way out of the egg) and immediately starts to feed on the food plant. As it grows larger, it has to moult (shed its skin) because caterpillar skins cannot stretch.

The female butterfly lays her eggs on the plant that she knows her caterpillar likes to eat.

When fully grown, the caterpillar finds a stem where it can turn into a chrysalis. It fixes itself to the stem with silk and then its skin splits and shrivels away to reveal the chrysalis.

How to use this book

To identify a butterfly you don't recognize, like the two shown here, follow these steps.

1 **Draw a quick sketch of the butterfly** (see page 23) in your field notebook. Draw the outline first, then fill in any other features you notice. Write down where and when you spotted the butterfly.

2 **Decide what habitat you are in.** Read the description at the start of each section, to see which one fits where you are. Each habitat has a different picture band.

3 **Look through the section with this picture band.** The picture and information given for each butterfly will help you identify it. The brightly patterned butterfly shown to the right is a Peacock (see page 14).

4 **If you can't find the butterfly there**, look through the other sections. Some butterflies can live in a wide variety of habitats.

5 **Sometimes, the females look different from the males**, like this Common Blue (see right and page 11). Make sure you study the pictures and the text carefully. The male ($\male$) and female ($\female$) wings are shown for each species.

6 **What month is it?** Many butterflies are seen only at certain times of the year. See the fact caption for each butterfly.

7 **If you still can't find the butterfly**, you may have to look in a larger field guide (see page 78 for some suggestions). You may have seen a very rare butterfly! Or it might be a moth (see page 59).

($\male$)   ($\female$)

When the adult inside the chrysalis is fully formed, the chrysalis splits and a soft, damp butterfly crawls out. The butterfly inflates its wings, lets them dry, and then flies off in search of nectar.

Habitat Picture Bands

This book is divided into different habitats (or types of countryside). Each habitat has a different picture band at the top of the page. These are shown below.

Farms, Parks & Gardens

Bogs & Marshes

Heath, Scrub & Valleys

Meadows

Mountains

Woodlands

5

What To Look For

Parts of a butterfly

Like all insects, a typical adult butterfly has three parts to its body, and three pairs of legs. The three body parts are the head, the thorax and the abdomen.

Each butterfly has two pairs of wings: two forewings and two hindwings. The wings are covered in scales, which give them their colour. When trying to identify a butterfly, check the following:

- Is it large or small?
- What colour and shape are its wings?
- Do they have patterns on them?
- Don't forget to look under the wings, as the colour and patterns there may be completely different.
- What are the antennae like?

The head has a pair of antennae, which are club-shaped at the tip, and a pair of big eyes, called compound eyes.

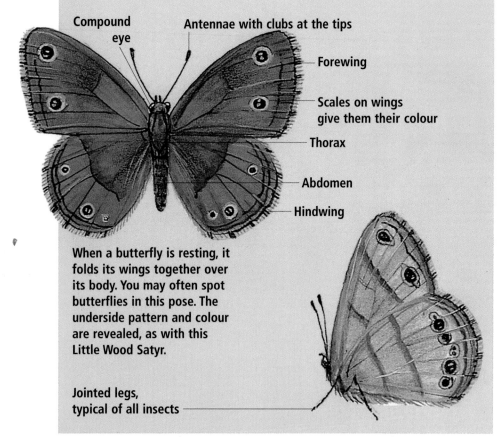

Compound eye

Antennae with clubs at the tips

Forewing

Scales on wings give them their colour

Thorax

Abdomen

Hindwing

When a butterfly is resting, it folds its wings together over its body. You may often spot butterflies in this pose. The underside pattern and colour are revealed, as with this Little Wood Satyr.

Jointed legs, typical of all insects

Wing shapes

The wing shapes of butterflies vary from rounded to triangular, to long and thin. Some wings have 'tails' on them; others have wavy edges.

The Holly Blue's hindwings are rounded and fringed (page 11)

The Two-tailed Pasha (page 74) has two tails on its hindwings

The Comma's hindwings have wavy edges (page 14)

The Small Skipper's wings are triangular in shape (page 16)

Antennae

Looking at a butterfly's antennae is a useful way to identify it as antennae vary from family to family.

All Skippers have antennae that hook outwards

The Small Apollo's antennae are stripy

6

Families of Butterflies

Colour & markings

The colour and markings (or patterns) on a butterfly's wings are one of the first things that you'll notice about it.

The Swallowtail (page 54) has orange and black marks on its hindwings called 'eyespots'. These look like eyes and frighten away would-be predators.

Male butterflies often have a black mark on the forewing, like the one on this Large Skipper (page 19).

The Silver-washed Fritillary (page 17) has a very noticeable pattern of black dots, dashes and crescents on orange.

Swallowtails, Apollos & Festoons

These butterflies are quite large, and lively fliers. The 'true' Swallowtails (see left) are all brightly coloured and have tails on their hindwings.

Apollos (see page 61) and Festoons are smaller and have no tails.

Whites & Yellows

Butterflies in this group are medium-sized, and are often white or yellow. Some of them have bright orange tips to their wings. Males and females often look quite different, as do these Green-veined whites (see page 20).

Skippers

These are among the smallest butterflies, and also the most numerous in Europe. The name 'Skipper' comes from the way that they fly – with a rapid, skipping movement. Like this Grizzled Skipper (see page 45), they have very distinctive hooked antennae, and also quite hairy bodies and triangular wings.

Brush Footed Butterflies

This is a very large group of butterflies. They are often medium-sized. The feature that really ties them together is the fact that they don't have six 'working' legs like other butterflies. Their forelegs are small and are of no use for walking. They are usually fast fliers.

They include the Browns and Ringlets (Satyridae), which are usually some shade of brown; the Fritillaries; the 'aristocrats' – Emperors, Admirals, Pashas, etc.; and the Snouts and Monarchs.

Blues, Coppers, Hairstreaks & Metalmarks

These butterflies are usually small and colourful, and like wild flowers. Blues, like this Large Blue (see page 10), are usually blue; while the Coppers are usually copper-coloured.

The Hairstreaks usually have small tails and a fine line crossing the underside of the hindwing.

Metalmarks, like the Duke of Burgundy Fritillary (page 52), get their name for the shiny, metallic markings on the wings of many tropical species.

Farms, Parks & Gardens

Some butterflies feed on very common plants like daisies, and these are the ones that you are most likely to see without too much hunting. You may well see the butterflies from this section in the other habitats covered in this book – meadows, mountains, woodlands, bogs and wetlands. Butterflies from those sections may also live in other types of landscape.

Roadsides in the country and the edges of fields are good places to spot butterflies, as there are often wild flowers growing there for them to visit. So next time you go for a drive in the country, or even along a busy road, keep a lookout for butterflies on the grassy edges.

Parks and gardens are ideal places to spot butterflies. They are filled with colourful flowers just perfect for sipping nectar from, and leaves just waiting to be nibbled by hungry caterpillars. A more unlikely habitat is waste ground, but it often gives a home to lots of butterflies. Waste ground includes railway yards and vacant plots of land which often have fast-growing weeds and hardy wild flowers growing through cracks in the concrete. The butterflies feed on very familiar weeds, such as buddleias, docks and daisies. This picture shows eight species from this section; how many can you recognize?

Red Admiral, Common Blue, Wall Brown, Comma, Silver-washed Fritillary, Peacock, Large Chequered Skipper, Green-veined White.

Marbled White

♂♀

♂

This butterfly is easy to recognize with its striking black and white colouring. The top of the wings have a black background with white spots. Their undersides have a similar pattern, but are not so brightly marked and have a yellowish tinge. You'll find the Marbled White flying in the summer, in open grassy areas, sipping nectar from flowers. The caterpillars are green, which camouflages them well against the grasses on which they feed.

Species: *Melanargia galathea*
Family: Satyridae
Size: Up to 54 mm
Flight period: One; flies in June and July
Distribution: Southern and Central Europe: not Scotland or Ireland

Grayling

This large butterfly has light brown wings, with light orange areas. There are two eyespots on the forewings, and one on each hindwing. Underneath, the wings have a complex pattern which gives excellent camouflage against the ground and also the bark of trees. There are also eyespots on the undersides, which makes it even more difficult for predators to catch them. Graylings live in grassy areas and near coastal cliffs. The straw-coloured caterpillars feed on different types of grasses.

♂♀   ♀

Species: *Hipparchia semele*
Family: Satyridae
Size: Up to 50 mm
Flight period: One; flies between May and August
Distribution: Most of Europe; not in northern Scandinavia

Large Blue

♂♀

♂

Species: *Maculinea arion*
Family: Lycaenidae
Size: Up to 40 mm
Flight period: One; flies in June and July
Distribution: Most of Europe, but not far north, Scotland, Wales or Ireland

This butterfly has bright blue wings with black spots on the upper forewing. Females have larger black spots than males. A dark band outlines the wings, enclosed by a white fringe. Underneath, the wings are light brown with dark spots and a bluish tinge at the base of the hindwings. The Large Blue can be seen on grassy hillsides, but it is very rare. At first, their caterpillars feed on thyme plants, and then they are carried off by ants into their nests. Here, the ants suck a milky liquid from the caterpillars, while the caterpillars feed on the ant grubs.

Holly Blue

This little butterfly has rounded wings, which are lilac blue. Females look different because they have broad black borders on their wings. Underneath, both males and females are a delicate blue colour, with little black spots. The Holly Blue can be seen fluttering around bushes and trees in waysides, clearings and gardens. Holly Blue caterpillars are unusual because they feed on different plants at different times of the year: holly in spring and ivy in the autumn.

Species: *Celastrina argiolus*
Family: Lycaenidae
Size: Up to 32 mm
Flight period: Two; flies in April/May and June/July
Distribution: Most of Europe except northern Scandinavia

Long-tailed Blue

So-called because of the long 'tails' on its wings, males of this butterfly are a bright violet colour. Females are less bright and have brown hindwings. Eyespots on the base of the hindwings confuse hungry predators. The undersides of the wings are mottled with wavy lines. The Long-tailed Blue flies in flowery meadows. Its caterpillars feed on plants in the pea family, and sometimes eat each other.

Species: *Lampides boeticus*
Family: Lycaenidae
Size: Up to 36 mm
Flight period: Three; flies between May and September
Distribution: Southern Europe, migrates occasionally to Britain

Common Blue

Male and female Common Blues hardly look like the same butterfly at all. The males have bright blue wings that glint in the sun, while females usually have brown wings with a row of orange spots around the margins. Both males and females have white outlines around their wings, and the undersides are light brown and speckled. The Common Blue, as its name suggests, can be easily spotted, especially in flowery meadows and open grassy areas. Caterpillars feed on vetches and clover.

Species: *Polyommatus icarus*
Family: Lycaenidae – **Size:** Up to 36 mm
Flight period: Three; flies between April and September
Distribution: All of Europe

Lang's Short-tailed Blue

Males of this butterfly have violet wings, while females have grey-brown wings. There is a little tail on the end of each hindwing, as well as two spots. Underneath, the wings are mottled brown and cream. Look for this butterfly flying in flowery areas. Caterpillars feed on plants in the pea family.

Species: *Leptotes pirithous*
Family: Lycaenidae
Size: Up to 26 mm
Flight period: Two; flies between March and July
Distribution: Southern Europe

Little Blue

♂♀ ♂

This is indeed a little butterfly, and is often called the 'Small Blue'. Both males and females have dark brown wings, and males have a blue tinge on their wings. The undersides of the wings are pale, with black spots and blue bases. Caterpillars, which are yellow, feed on kidney vetch flowers. Look for the Little Blue flitting from flower to flower in grassy areas and on cliffs by the coast.

Species: *Cupido minimus*
Family: Lycaenidae – Size: Up to 24 mm
Flight period: Two; flies between April and September
Distribution: Most of Europe, except the extreme north and south

Ringlet

This butterfly gets its name from the string of ringed eyespots along the undersides of the wings. On top, the ringlet is a dark brown, with two spots on each fore- and hindwing. You can tell the females by their slightly paler colour. Look for the Ringlet in wet grassy places, such as ditches or woodland glades and edges, also in hedgerows. Caterpillars feed on grass during the night.

♂♀ ♂

Species: *Aphantopus hyperantus*
Family: Satyridae
Size: Up to 48 mm
Flight period: One; flies between June and August
Distribution: All of Europe, except far north and far south

Oberthur's Grizzled Skipper

This little butterfly has soft brown wings with lighter markings. Underneath, the hindwings are reddish brown and covered in vivid light marks. The forewing undersides are black with a definite spot on each wing. Look for this butterfly on flowery slopes.

♂♀ ♂

Species: *Pyrgus armoricanus*
Family: Hesperiidae
Size: Up to 28 mm
Flight period: Two; flies between May and September
Distribution: Central and Southern Europe

Large Chequered Skipper

This butterfly may look dull above, with its plain brown colouring, but a flash of its undersides reveals a garish pattern of big white spots on a yellow background. The upper forewings have some tiny marks, and females have chequered black and white fringes around their wings. This butterfly lives in waysides and meadows, and can be seen in the summer. Its caterpillars feed on grasses.

Species: *Heteropterus morpheus*
Family: Hesperiidae
Size: Up to 38 mm
Flight period: One; flies between June and July
Distribution: Northern Spain, central and southern Europe

♂♀ ♂

Meadow Brown

Females of this butterfly boast a more colourful pattern and a larger size than the males. They are brown with a big orange patch on each forewing, as well as a large eyespot. Males are all brown, with only a hint of orange on the forewings, and much smaller eyespots. Underneath, the wings are paler in colour, with a light band. As the name suggests, you can see this butterfly flying in grassy meadows or roadsides in the summer. Its caterpillars are green and yellow and feed on grasses.

Species: *Maniola jurtina*
Family: Satyridae – Size: Up to 50 mm
Flight period: Two; two to three generations per year; flies between June and September
Distribution: Most of Europe, except far north

Dusky Meadow Brown

Males of this butterfly are mostly brown, and have one or two eyespots on the forewings, as well as a dark streak. Females are larger, with two clearer spots on the forewings, as well as on the underside. Both males and females have dark hindwings, above and below. The Dusky Meadow Brown flies in grassy areas in the summer, and its caterpillars feed on meadow grasses.

Species: *Hyponephele lycaon*
Family: Satyridae
Size: Up to 48 mm
Flight period: One; flies between June and August
Distribution: Central and southern Europe

Large Wall Brown

This butterfly lives up to its name in every way: it is large, brown and often sits on walls, basking in the sun. The wings have a brown background, with orange and black markings, a large eyespot on each forewing, and two on each hindwing. Females have more orange markings than males. Underneath, the wings are patterned in silvery-grey, with a ring of eyespots on each hindwing. When not sunbathing on walls and rocks, this butterfly can be seen flying in grassy areas. Caterpillars feed on different types of grasses.

Species: *Lasiommata maera*
Family: Satyridae
Size: Up to 56 mm
Flight period: Two; flies between June and September
Distribution: Most of Europe, but not the British Isles

Farms, Parks & Gardens

Red Admiral

♂♀

♂

This handsome, large butterfly is hard to miss. It has bright red bars crossing its forewings, which are black at the top, and spotted with white. The hindwings have red bars on their borders. Underneath, the wings have a mottled pattern of black, brown and blue. The Red Admiral flies around flowery areas, hedgerows, woodland clearings and gardens. It likes to drink water from puddles and sap from trees, and will also drink juice from rotting fruit in the autumn. Caterpillars feed on nettle leaves.

Species: *Vanessa atalanta*
Family: Nymphalidae – Size: Up to 64 mm
Flight period: One; flies between May and October
Distribution: All of Europe

Peacock

The trademarks of this beautiful butterfly are the four big eyespots on its wings. They are set against a rich red-brown background, and there are also shades of blue, black, white and yellow. A dark margin surrounds the wings, and underneath, they are almost black. Sunshine lovers, Peacocks sip nectar and sunbathe along waysides, in glades and in gardens. If threatened by predators, they flash their coloured eyespots. Caterpillars are black and hairy, and feed on nettle leaves.

Species: *Inachis io* – Family: Nymphalidae – Size: Up to 60 mm
Flight period: One; flies between March and September
Distribution: Most of Europe; not the extreme north

♂♀

♂

Comma

♂♀

♂

With its ragged outline, the Comma is well camouflaged against leaves and tree bark. Its wings are patterned with orange and brown on top, and brown underneath, with the white 'comma' mark that gives it its name on the hindwing. Comma caterpillars look like bird droppings to avoid being eaten by predators. They feed on hop leaves and nettles. Look for the Comma on sunny days, sipping nectar from flowers in gardens, on farmland and on roadsides.

Species: *Polygonia c-album*
Family: Nymphalidae – Size: Up to 48 mm
Flight period: Two; flies between March and July
Distribution: Most of Europe, but not Scotland or Ireland

Gatekeeper

You will find this orange-brown butterfly around country hedgerows in the summer. Males are smaller than females, and have a deeper orange colour. They also have a dark streak along the forewings. Both males and females have eyespots on the forewings to confuse predators. Gatekeepers sip nectar from marjoram, wood sage, valerian and bramble flowers. Their caterpillars feed on various types of grasses.

Species: *Pyronia tithonus*
Family: Satyridae
Size: Up to 40 mm
Flight period; One: flies between June and September
Distribution: Southern and Central Europe, but not Scotland

Chestnut Heath

This butterfly's name comes from the chestnut colour of its forewings, which is much lighter in the females. The forewings are chestnut underneath, too. The hindwings are brown and have a row of dark eyespots underneath. The Chestnut Heath flies in grassy areas in the summer. Caterpillars feed on grasses.

Species: *Coenonympha glycerion*
Family: Satyriidae – **Size:** Up to 36 mm
Flight period: One – flies between June and July
Distribution:
Northern Spain,
central/southern
France, from the
Alps eastwards

Dark Green Fritillary

This butterfly gets its name not from its upper colour, but from the colour underneath its hindwing. On top, it is orange-brown with black markings. The underside colour is the best way to identify this butterfly. Look for the silvery spots on the green background. The Dark Green Fritillary flits quickly between flowers in glades, and on waysides and heaths. Caterpillars feed on violet leaves.

Species: *Argynnis aglaja*
Family: Nymphalidae – **Size:** Up to 58 mm
Flight period: One; flies between June and August
Distribution: Most of Europe

Pallas's Fritillary

This butterfly's tiger-like colouring and markings make it easy to spot. Its wings are bright orange with black marks. Underneath, the hindwings are greenish on the inside and reddish on the outside. Pallas's Fritillary can be seen flying along flowery waysides and in glades in the summer. Its caterpillars feed on bog violets.

Species: *Argynnis laodice*
Family: Nymphalidae
Size: Up to 58 mm
Flight period: One;
flies between July
and August
Distribution:
Eastern Europe
eastwards
Very rare: habitat mainly
damp woodland

Essex Skipper

♂♀   ♂

This butterfly is so-called because it was first identified in Essex, England. It has orange-brown wings outlined in black, and males have a dark streak on their forewings. Underneath, the wings are dusky brown-green. The best way to identify this butterfly is to look for the black tips on the underside of the antennae. The Essex Skipper flies quickly in grassy areas, meadows and roadsides, where its caterpillars feed on blades of grass.

Species: *Thymelicus lineola*
Family: Hesperiidae – Size: Up to 28 mm
Flight period: One; flies between May and August
Distribution: Central and southern Europe, but in the British Isles, only in Southern England

Small Skipper

♂♀   ♂

You might think at first glance that this was an Essex Skipper, but look again. The Small Skipper does not have black tips on the underside of its antennae. Apart from this, the two are almost exactly the same. The wings are orange-brown with a black outline. Underneath they are paler. Males have a dark streak on their forewings, longer than that of the Essex Skipper. The Small Skipper can be seen in the summer, flying swiftly through grassy meadows, sipping the nectar of wild flowers. Its caterpillars feed on grass.

Species: *Thymelicus sylvestris*
Family: Hesperiidae
Size: Up to 32 mm
Flight period: One; flies between June and August
Distribution: Most of Europe, except far north, Scotland and Ireland

Marbled Fritillary

This butterfly's rounded wings are orange, speckled with black marks. The undersides of the hindwings are yellowish towards the body, graduating to purplish on the outer edge. Females are bigger than males. The Marbled Fritillary flies mainly in open woodland and in flowery waysides, on both lowland and upland. Its caterpillars feed on bramble.

♂♀

Species: *Brenthis daphne*
Family: Nymphalidae
Size: Up to 54 mm
Flight period:
One; flies between
June and August
Distribution: South
and Central Europe

Lesser Fiery Copper

This butterfly is so-called because of the fiery orange colour to the wings. Males have orange forewings, and paler hindwings with a row of black marks. Females are slightly different, with forewings and hindwings covered in black marks. Underneath, the hindwings are white-grey and speckled with black spots and an orange band around the edge. The Lesser Fiery Copper likes scrub and waste ground and light woodlands. Its caterpillars feed on docks and broom.

♂♀   ♂

Species: *Lycaena thersamon*
Family: Lycaenidae – Size: Up to 32 mm
Flight period: Two; flies between April and August
Distribution: Italy and eastern Europe

Silky Ringlet

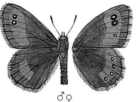 

♂♀   ♀

This butterfly is brown, with a wide band of orange crossing the forewing and part of the hindwing. In males, the band is red-orange with two black eyespots with white pupils. In females, the band is lighter orange with an extra spot on the forewing and four more spots on the hindwing. Underneath, the forewings are yellow-brown, with two eyespots, and the hindwings are mottled grey-brown. The Silky Ringlet flies on rocky slopes in mountains. Its caterpillars feed on grasses.

Species: *Erebia gorge* – **Family:** Satyridae – **Size:** Up to 40 mm
Flight period: One; flies between June and August
Distribution: Scattered through central and southern Europe

Mountain Ringlet

This dark coloured butterfly has dark brown wings crossed by a red-orange band across the forewing. Within this band are black spots. There are also some orange spots around the hindwing margin. The underside hindwing is pale brown, while the forewing has an orange base. It is found in mountainous, often boggy areas, where it flies close to the ground. Look for this butterfly in sunny weather in alpine grassy meadows. When the sun goes in, it hides in the grass. Caterpillars feed on grasses – especially mat and wavy-haired grasses.

Species: *Erebia epiphron* – **Family:** Satyridae
Size: Up to 38 mm – **Flight period:** One; flies between June and August – **Distribution:** Mountains of central and southern Europe, including Britain

♀

♂♀

Hermit

This butterfly has brown wings crossed by a white-cream band running vertically down each side. There are two dark spots on the forewings, but these are more definite in the female, and they also have white 'pupils'. Females can also be recognized by their larger size. The Hermit flies in rocky places and along rocky paths.

Species: *Chazara briseis*
Family: Satyridae
Size: Up to 60 mm
Flight period: One; flies between June and July
Distribution: South and central Europe

♂♀

Great Sooty Satyr

The name 'Sooty' suits the males of this butterfly much better than the females. Males have very dark brown wings with two black, white-pupilled eyespots on the forewings. Females are orange-brown, with two much larger pupilled eyespots on their forewings, as well as one on the hindwing. Look for the Great Sooty Satyr in the summer, flying on dry mountain slopes and tracks. The caterpillars feed on tufted hair-grass, plentiful in these areas.

Species: *Satyrus ferula*
Family: Satyridae
Size: Up to 60 mm
Flight period: One; flies between July and August
Distribution: Southern Europe rarely north of 47°N

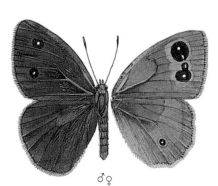

♂♀

Mountains

Marbled Skipper

♂♀   ♂

This butterfly is so-called because of the marbled pattern on its wings, which are greenish grey with white marks on fore- and hindwings. The undersides of the wings are pale green with very light bands, and the hindwings have a scalloped margin. The Marbled Skipper lives in flowery areas of slopes. Here, its caterpillars feed on woundwort.

Species: *Carcharodus lavatherae*
Family: Hesperiidae
Size: Up to 28 mm
Flight period: Two; flies between May and August
Distribution: Central and southern Europe

Tufted Marbled Skipper

This butterfly's name tells you a lot about its appearance. The male has hair tufts on the underside of its forewings, and its pattern on top is marbled with green, white, orange and black. Underneath, the hindwings are greenish with white marks, and the forewings are brownish. This skipper flies on flowery slopes, and its caterpillars' foodplant is white horehound.

Species: *Carcharodus flocciferus*
Family: Hesperiidae – **Size:** Up to 32 mm
Flight period: Two; flies between May and September
Distribution: Southern and central Europe

♂♀   ♂

Hungarian Skipper

As the name hints, this butterfly can be found in Eastern Europe. The Hungarian Skipper has brown wings, with a fine line of white dashes inside the margins. Underneath, the wings are pale olive-green with large white spots. It flies on flowery slopes, where its caterpillars feed on burnets and cinquefoils.

Species: *Spialia orbifer*
Family: Hesperiidae
Size: Up to 30 mm
Flight period: Two; flies between April and August
Distribution: Eastern Europe

♂♀   ♂

Chequered Blue

This butterfly has two 'chequered' areas. There are chequered fringes on its wings, and its undersides have an overall chequered pattern. Above, the males have dark blue forewings with a brown margin and brown hindwings. Females are brown with dark markings. The undersides of the wings are grey-white covered in large blocks of black. The hindwing also has a row of orange half-moon shapes. The Chequered Blue flies on rocky ground in the summer. Its caterpillars feed on stonecrop.

♂♀   ♂

Species: *Scolitantides orion*
Family: Lycaenidae
Size: Up to 32 mm
Flight period: Two; flies between April and August
Distribution: Two distinct areas: Spain eastwards through southern and central Europe, and southern Scandinavia

Painted Lady

This big, handsome butterfly has pointed forewings with black tips filled with white marks. There are also orange marks on the forewings, and the hindwings are orange and brown with a row of black spots and dashes around the margin. The undersides of the wings are rosy on the forewing and have a marbled pattern on the hindwing, with five eyespots. It can also be recognized by its flight – very fast and powerful, covering large distances. It flies over meadows, hedgerows and gardens, settling to sip nectar. Caterpillars feed on the leaves of thistles, mallows, burdock and stinging nettles.

Species: *Vanessa cardui* – Family: Nymphalidae
Size: Up to 70 mm
Flight period: Three; flies between April and October as a migrant
Distribution: Most of Europe in summer; one of the world's most widespread butterflies

Spanish Purple Hairstreak

This butterfly has dark brown wings, and males boast a substantial purple area on their forewings. Females only have a little purple on their wings. Underneath, the wings are very different, light tan, with spotted orange borders. The hindwings have scalloped edges. This hairstreak is common in Spain, where it flies in woodland areas in mountains. Caterpillars feed on ash leaves.

Species: *Laeosopis roboris* – Family: Lycaenidae
Size: Up to 30 mm
Flight period: One; flies between May and July
Distribution: Portugal, Spain and southern France

Sooty Ringlet

The very sooty-black wings of the males give this butterfly its name. Sometimes these black wings have two tiny pupilled spots on the forewings and two on the hindwing. Females have dark brown wings, with a very faint lighter brown band running down them. Underneath, the wings are sooty and plain. The Sooty Ringlet lives in mountainous areas, where its caterpillars can feed on sparse-growing meadow grasses.

Species: *Erebia pluto* – Family: Satyridae – Size: Up to 50 mm
Flight period: One; flies between June and August
Distribution: Alps and Apennines

Keeping Records

You might like to keep a diary recording when and where you find your butterflies. Always take your field notebook with you when you go butterfly hunting. Make sketches of the butterflies you see for your diary, and take photographs of the area.

Butterfly diary

Keep your diary in a ring binder or a lever-arch file on separate sheets of paper. Fill out a sheet for each butterfly-hunting trip you go on with the details from your field notebook.

You can also write notes in it when you visit museums, or see a television programme about butterflies. You can decorate it with your own drawings, photographs, pictures from magazines, postcards and so on.

Butterfly walk

A good way to find out about butterflies in your neighbourhood is by going on a regular 'butterfly walk'. This is how to do it:

1 **Plan a route that takes about one hour to walk** (about 4–5 km). Make sure it takes you past the different habitats in your neighbourhood (like fields, woods, lakes, parks, etc).

2 **Try to take this walk once a week** during the warmest time of the day and to do it in about one hour on each occasion. Try not to do it when the weather is wet or windy.

3 **Take your field notebook and this guidebook each time.**

4 **Record each butterfly** that comes within five metres of you, and how many there are.

Keeping a record

You can also record each species of butterfly that you see in a card index. The file should have a card for each species that gives detailed information like:

- the butterfly's common name, and its Latin name if known
- the family to which it belongs
- the date you saw it
- where you saw it: name and description of place
- the type of habitat
- the weather on the day of your visit

You may be able to store your information on a computer. Keep an up-to-date printout, as well as your disk and its back-up.

5 **If you have to stop and identify a butterfly you don't recognize**, don't worry. Make a note of the time it takes you to identify the butterfly and add that time to the one hour your walk should take.

6 **Record your weekly information in a separate part of your butterfly diary.** Over the weeks, you will see which areas are best for butterflies and which species are most common at what time of year. Does your local pattern match the flight time information in this book?

Make a butterfly kite

Butterflies are so beautiful, they have inspired artists for centuries. Thousands of years ago, kite-makers in China made butterfly kites to flutter in the wind. You can make your own butterfly kite with some strong paper, two straws, some thin string, Sellotape and paints or markers.

1 **Draw an outline of a butterfly on a piece of paper.** Colour in the wings with your paints or markers, giving them whatever pattern you like.

2 **When dry, cut the shape out from the paper**, being careful to keep it in one piece.

3 **Make some antennae from the string** and glue them to the butterfly's head.

4 **Place a long piece of string against the butterfly's body.** Lay the straws diagonally across the wings, on top of the string.

5 **Tape the straws down firmly** on to each of the four wing tips.

6 **Tie the string and the straws together** over the middle of the butterfly. Now your kite is ready to fly!

67

Woodlands

The woodland habitat includes two quite different types of woods. Deciduous, broad-leaved woods and forests are made up of trees that lose their leaves in winter, such as oak, beech, and ash. These trees have broad, flat leaves. Coniferous woods and forests are green all year round, and include pines, firs, cypresses and cedars. These trees have needle-like leaves.

Coniferous forests, which occur mostly in the northern parts of Europe, have few flowers growing on their floors because their thickly-packed branches let in so little sunshine. So you will not find many butterflies in this type of habitat.

Deciduous woodlands and forests are more common in the rest of Europe. They let in plenty of light during the springtime to allow lots of wild flowers to grow on their floors. Here, you'll find butterflies drinking nectar, or resting on twigs and branches in sunny clearings (gaps among the trees). Don't forget to look for caterpillars munching on leaves and plants as well.

Clearings are found in both types of forest. They can be caused by the fall of a great tree that is at the end of its life, or by the actions of humans. The gap in the forest roof lets in sunlight and fast-growing plants take advantage of this before the slower-growing saplings shoot up to fill the hole. This picture shows four species from this section; how many can you recognize?

White Admiral, Black-eyed Blue, Brown Hairstreak, Purple Hairstreak.

Woodlands

Woodland Grayling

This big butterfly is ideally coloured for its woodland habitat. On top, the wings are brown, with a wide, lighter area towards the margins, and eyespots on the forewings. In females, this is yellowish towards the forewing margin and the eyespots are stronger. Underneath, the hindwing has a wavy pattern very like bark and perfect for camouflage. Caterpillars of the Woodland Grayling feed on a grass called Yorkshire Fog.

Species: *Hipparchia fagi* – **Family: Satyridae**
Size: Up to 76 mm
Flight period: One; flies between June and August
Distribution: South and central Europe

Purple Emperor

A big, spectacular butterfly, the Purple Emperor gets its name from the bright purple sheen on the male's wings. They also have a black border and white marks. Females have light brown wings with white marks. Underneath, the wings are patterned with orange, white and brown marks. They fly in clearings, mostly in the treetops, particularly among oak trees. Because of this, you'll find it hard to spot one, except in the morning sipping nectar from flowers on woodland paths. Caterpillars are fat and green – they feed on willow leaves.

Species: *Apatura iris* – **Family: Nymphalidae**
Size: Up to 75 mm
Flight period: One; flies between July and August
Distribution: Most of Europe, except far north and south – not in Scotland or Ireland

Lesser Purple Emperor

To confuse you, there are two colour forms of this butterfly. One has a yellowish brown tinge, while the other is similar to the Purple Emperor. In the latter form, males have the purple sheen on their wings, white markings and an orange-ringed black spot on the forewing. Females are brown, with white marks and orange and black spots on the forewing. The Lesser Purple Emperor flies along woodland paths and in clearings, where its caterpillars feed on poplar and willow leaves.

Species: *Apatura ilia*
Family: Nymphalidae
Size: Up to 70 mm
Flight period: Two; flies between May and September
Distribution: Central and southern Europe, but not Britain, Mediterranean lowlands or most of Spain

Black-eyed Blue

Males and females of this butterfly look slightly different. The males have plain blue wings with thin black margins. The females have blue wings too, but they have a lot of black in them seeping in from the margins and darkening the blue colour. Underneath, males and females have grey coloured wings, with a row of large black dots, especially on the forewings. The Black-eyed Blue flies on heaths and in woods in the spring. Its caterpillars feed on greenwood, leopard's bane and birdsfoot trefoil.

Species: *Glaucopsyche melanops*
Family: Lycaenidae – Size: Up to 32 mm
Flight period: One; flies in April and May
Distribution: Southwest Europe

Iolas Blue

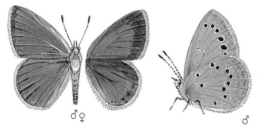

Males of this large blue have violet-blue wings with thin dark margins. Females have darker blue wings with wider dark margins. Undersides are fawn with a row of white ringed black spots. The Iolas Blue flies in scrubby areas and in light woodland where its caterpillars can find their food plant, bladder senna.

Species: *Iolana iolas* – Family: Lycaenidae – Size: Up to 42 mm
Flight period: Two; flies between May and September
Distribution: Southern and eastern Europe

Purple Hairstreak

The name of this butterfly suits the males more than the females. They have bright purple all over their wings, with dark margins. Females have brown wings with just a small area of purple on the forewings. The undersides of males and females are the same, silvery grey with a white 'hairstreak', an orange spot and a tiny tail. There are also 'watermarks' on the margins of the hindwing. Purple Hairstreaks live in woodlands, but you'll have to look hard to find them, as they live in the tops of oak trees, rarely descending to a pathway or clearing. They are very territorial, and will attack any intruder. Rather than taking nectar from flowers, they sip honeydew left by aphids on leaves. Caterpillars feed mainly on oak leaves.

Species: *Quercusia quercus*
Family: Lycaenidae – Size: Up to 30 mm
Flight period: One; flies between June and September
Distribution: Most of Europe except northern Scandinavia

Common Glider

White bands cross the wings of this butterfly on a black background. The pattern is the same on the underside, although the hindwing has a reddish tinge. The Common Glider flies in woodlands and scrubby hillsides, glades and clearings. Its caterpillars are smooth with four pairs of spiny projections on the back, they eat spring pea.

Species: *Neptis sappho*
Family: Nymphalidae
Size: Up to 50 mm
Flight period: Two; flies between May and September
Distribution: Eastern central Europe

Woodlands

Scotch Argus

♂♀ ♀

Large Ringlet

♂♀

In the British Isles, the Scotch Argus lives mainly in Scotland, but elsewhere in Europe it is widespread. Dark brown wings crossed with orange bands are its trademark. The bands are filled with black, white-centred eyespots. This pattern is repeated on the forewing underside, and on the hindwing there is a grey band with small white dots. The Scotch Argus lives on woodland edges, in forest glades and rides, and on moorland. A sun-loving butterfly, you'll find it hard to spot one if the sun is not out. When at rest, the Scotch Argus looks like a withered leaf and so avoids attack. Caterpillars feed on grasses.

Species: *Erebia aethiops* – Family: Satyridae
Size: Up to 40 mm
Flight period: One; flies between July and September
Distribution: Scotland and central, southeastern and eastern Europe

This butterfly has rich brown wings with an orange band crossing them, filled with a row of black spots. Females are a bit bigger and their black spots have white pupils. Underneath, the pattern is the same but paler, with chequered margins. Look for the Large Ringlet flying on mountain slopes and in clearings and woodland in the summer. Caterpillars feed on different types of grasses.

Species: *Erebia euryale*
Family: Satyridae
Size: Up to 48 mm
Flight period: One; flies between July and August
Distribution: From northern Spain to southeastern Europe, via the Alps

♂

Woodland Brown

This butterfly lives up to its name, as its wings are brown, and it lives in woodlands. The wings are large with scalloped, chequered margins and a row of yellow-ringed spots running vertically down each wing. Females have larger spots. On the underside, the pattern is repeated, with two yellow lines around the margins. It lives in and around open woodland, in glades and clearings. Caterpillars feed on grasses.

Woodland Ringlet

This butterfly is brown, with a row of eyespots set in orange running down its wings. In males, this pattern is repeated very strongly on the underside. Females are similar, but larger and paler with larger eyespots above. The Woodland Ringlet flies on moors, and in meadows, bogs and light woodland. Caterpillars feed on finger grass and wood millet.

Species: *Erebia medusa*
Family: Satyridae
Size: Up to 48 mm
Flight period: One; flies between May and June
Distribution: Central and eastern Europe

Species: *Lopina achine*
Family: Satyridae
Size: Up to 56 mm
Flight period: One; flies between May and August
Distribution: Central Europe

♂♀

♂♀

♀

72

Ilex Hairstreak

This butterfly is named after the food plant of its caterpillars, the holm or ilex oak. Males and females look different. The males have brown wings, with a small orange spot at the rear of the hindwing. Females are brighter, with a large orange mark on the forewing as well. The hindwings have tails, and are crossed on the underside with a white hairstreak line and an orange band. The Ilex Hairstreak lives in lightly wooded areas.

Species: *Satyrium ilicis*
Family: Lycaenidae – Size: Up to 36 mm
Flight period: One; flies between June and July
Distribution: Southern and central Europe

False Ilex Hairstreak

Males and females of this butterfly both have rich brown wings. Females lack the bright orange mark of the Ilex Hairstreak, and have only a faint smudge on their forewings. There are tiny tails on the hindwings, and underneath, a row of orange spots around the margin. Look for this butterfly in light woodland and scrubby areas.

Species: *Satyrium esculi*
Family: Lycaenidae
Size: Up to 34 mm
Flight period: One;
flies between
June and August
Distribution:
Southwestern Europe

White-letter Hairstreak

You can only see the reason for this butterfly's name by looking on the underside of the hindwing. Here, there is a letter 'W' in white, as well as orange and black marks. Above, the wings are plain dark brown with tails on the hindwings. The White-letter Hairstreak lives in light woodland areas and around trees in towns. It sips nectar from bramble and privet blossom. Caterpillars feed on the leaves and flowers of elm trees. Dutch Elm Disease has had a devastating effect on this species, but it still survives.

Species: *Satyrium w-album*
Family: Lycaenidae
Size: Up to 32 mm
Flight period: One; flies in July
Distribution: Mos of Europe, except
the far north – not in Scotland or Ireland

Brown Hairstreak

Both males and females of this butterfly have brown wings with little tails on the hindwings. Females are much brighter however, with broad bands of orange crossing their forewings, as well as orange on the tails. The Brown Hairstreak lives in woodlands and hedgerow trees, feeding on honeydew left on leaves by aphids. It is hard to spot, because it stays high in the treetops. Caterpillars feed on sloe, plum and birch leaves.

Species: *Thecla betulae*
Family: Lycaenidae
Size: Up to 36 mm
Flight period: One;
flies between July and
September – Distribution:
Most of Europe, except
the far north – not Scotland or Ireland

73

Strength, timing and control

Each wrestling contest between two wrestlers is called a bout. There are many different forms of wrestling, but all of them involve a wrestler using his or her strength and timing to gain control over their opponent. This involves gripping the opponent and sometimes throwing them to the floor. Points are awarded for various techniques during the bout.

South Korea's Kim Min-chul lifts Rawshan Ruzikulov of Uzbekistan.

SEVEN IN A ROW

At the age of 47, ten years before he became the first ever President of the United States, George Washington won seven wrestling bouts in a row against opponents from the Massachusetts Volunteer army!

5

AN ANCIENT HISTORY

Wrestling is one of the world's oldest sports. Archaeologists have discovered paintings of wrestlers from ancient Egypt and ancient Babylonia (Iraq), some dating back over 5,000 years.

Jiao li

In China, Jiao li wrestling developed thousands of years ago. It is the oldest Chinese martial art. By 200 BCE, Jiao li wrestlers were bodyguards to the Emperor of China.

Pehlwani wrestling

Ancient Pehlwani (or Pehalwan) wrestling from India is more than 2,500 years old and is still performed today. In the first half of the twentieth century, the greatest Pehlwani wrestler was Ghulum Mohammed, known as the Great Gama. He lost only a single match in over 5,000 wrestling bouts!

Pehlwani wrestling practised by Pakistani wrestlers at an akhra – a traditional wrestlers training institute – in Pakistan.

6

ANCIENT OLYMPICS

The ancient Greeks were keen wrestlers, and from 708 BCE wrestling was an event at the ancient Olympics. Legends were created there including Milo of Kroton, who is said to have won the adult wrestling competition an incredible five times in a row. The Romans took on the Greek style of wrestling, creating the Greco-Roman style still in use today.

"I swear it upon Zeus, an outstanding runner cannot be the equal of an average wrestler." - *Socrates, famous Greek scholar.*

WRESTLING AROUND THE WORLD

Compared to many combat sports which began in just one country, wrestling developed all over the world. Many forms are still popular in one country or in a specific region.

Schwingen

In Switzerland, Schwingen wrestling (below) is centuries old. Wrestlers wear shorts over their clothes. The two wrestlers hold onto their opponent's shorts and try to throw each other onto their backs.

Sumo

Sumo wrestling (right) is hugely popular in Japan. Professional wrestlers try to force each other out of a circular ring, called a *dohyo*. They can also win a bout by forcing their opponent to touch the ground with a part of their body other than their feet. The very greatest sumo wrestlers are given the title *Yokozuna*.

Evala

Evala wrestling (left) occurs every year amongst the Kaybé people of northern Togo and signals a boy's progress into adulthood.

Sambo

Sambo is a form of self-defence invented in Russia. As a sport for men and women, a bout lasts six minutes. Sambo wrestlers wear a tight jacket called a *kurka* and shorts called *trusi*.

FOLK WRESTLING

Some forms of wrestling are known as folk wrestling. They are thousands of years old, but are still performed at festivals and competitions today.

Glima wrestling

The Vikings brought Glima wrestling to Iceland over 800 years ago. It involves both wrestlers wearing a special leather belt which their opponent grips. The two wrestlers have to stand upright and step around each other in a circle.

Cumberland and Westmoreland wrestling

This is believed to have been brought to England by the Vikings. It begins with the wrestlers linking their fingers behind the back of their opponent. This hold must be kept throughout the bout as the wrestlers struggle to throw their opponent.

These wrestlers are trying to throw each other to the ground.

10

Oiled up

Yagli Güres is a traditional form of wrestling from Turkey. Wrestlers wear leather shorts called *kispet* and cover their bodies in slippery olive oil. Originally, there were no time limits and bouts could last for two days! Today, bouts are either 30 or 40 minutes long.

The oil makes it more difficult to get a good hold on your opponent.

Modern folkstyle

Wrestling boomed in US schools and colleges and is now called folkstyle or collegiate wrestling. It is similar to freestyle wrestling (see page 12) and allows the use of legs and arms to make holds. It places more importance on control than making big throws.

11

WRESTLING TODAY

Today, two forms of wrestling dominate international competitions – Greco-Roman and freestyle wrestling. Both are amateur sports where competitors are not paid to perform.

These wrestlers are battling it out in the Greco-Roman wrestling 66 kg final at the European Wrestling Championships.

12

What's the difference?

The key difference is that in Greco-Roman wrestling, wrestlers are not allowed to attack the legs of their opponents. All their moves and holds must be at waist height or above. In freestyle wrestling, competitors are allowed to use their legs to attack and defend with. They can also grip and hold an opponent's legs.

These two wrestlers are taking part in a freestyle beach wrestling competition in France.

Weight classes

In both Greco-Roman and freestyle competitions, wrestlers are divided up according to their body weight. For male Olympic wrestling there are seven weight classes: up to 55kg, 55–60kg, 60–66kg, 66–74kg, 74–84kg, 84–96kg and 96–120kg.

KEEP ON GROWING

Hungary's Gyula Bobis began wrestling in one of the lightest weight classes. As he grew in size and weight, he moved up the weight classes. By the time he wrestled at the 1948 Olympics, aged 38, he was in the heaviest class and won the gold medal!

IN TRAINING

Wrestling requires complete body fitness. Successful wrestlers of all ages train hard to improve their fitness, strength, speed of movement and their wrestling techniques.

Preparation

Wrestling involves lots of twisting and turning to avoid an opponent's attacks, as well as to make attacks. This means that parts of the body need to be stretched before training begins.

Muscles need to be stretched before training.

Mat matters

An official wrestling mat is 9 metres in diameter and is surrounded by a 1.5 metre wide border. Wrestlers always train on a mat to avoid injury.

HARD FLOOR

When South Korea's Kim Young-nam began wrestling, his school could not afford wrestling mats. He trained and practised on a hard wooden floor covered in dried rice stalks. He went on to win a gold medal at the 1988 Olympics.

Kitted out

Wrestling equipment is very simple compared to other sports. An all-in-one outfit, called a singlet, is worn in competition. It is made of stretchy material and is usually either red or blue. In training, wrestlers may wear shorts and vests. Wrestling boots are lace-up with no heels and are made of soft leather. Many junior wrestlers wear a padded headguard.

These wrestlers at Pennsylvania High School, USA, are wearing protective headgear.

"The stamina that is needed is tremendous. I cross-train with weight workouts, mountain biking, running and any way that I can move my body." – Olympic wrestler Vickie Zummo on her training programme.

TOP 10 WRESTLING MOVES 1—3

A wrestling bout begins with the two competitors trying to get a good position to attack their opponent. Tie-ups can force an opponent into a weaker position from which a headlock may be possible. The aim of these moves is to then perform a takedown – a move which brings the opponent down onto the mat.

1 Double wrist tie-up

Tie-ups are grips or holds that help wrestlers move their opponents around. The double wrist tie-up sees a wrestler grip both of his opponent's wrists firmly.

The attacking wrestler can then try to unbalance his opponent by stepping to the side or forcing his opponent's arms down.

2 Underhook

In this tie-up move a wrestler grabs under his opponent's arm and holds on to the back of his shoulder. He can control his opponent easily, or move into another hold, called a bear hug. Having two underhooks on at the same time is called a double underhook.

3 Headlock

A headlock is a hold in which an arm is wrapped around the opponent's neck and the two hands are then locked together. The opponent's arm must be inside the loop created by the attacker's hands to stop any chances of choking. From this position, the attacker may be able to make a takedown move.

MIND AND BODY

Wrestling requires mental and physical fitness. A wrestler has to be alert and determined in order to succeed. According to Olympic gold medal winner, Kendal Cross, "You really have to work hard for something that doesn't always pay off immediately."

Listening and learning

Wrestlers learn and improve their skills by working hard and listening to every word their coach says. Discipline and focus help wrestlers to compete at their best.

"You have to train the mind and the body to function and excel while someone is trying to beat you up." – *Jim Gruenwald, Olympic wrestler.*

Young wrestlers, like these, learn from their more experienced coach.

Thinking tactics

"When your head is really into a match, time seems to slow right down," says Canadian wrestler Nick Ugoalah. He won a gold medal at the 2002 Commonwealth Games and was three-times Canadian wrestling champion. Top wrestlers keep thinking throughout a bout looking for a chance to win. As Ugoalah recalls, "All through a match, I'd be probing, testing, trying to find out what made my opponent uncomfortable."

Wrestlers usually train as part of a team or a club. Respect for others in your team is also an important part of wrestling.

A WINNING MIND

Bulgarian freestyle wrestler Valentin Jordanov was famous for being incredibly strong in his mind. He had a remarkable competition record. In 685 events he won 673!

PROFESSIONAL WRESTLING

Professional wrestling bouts have occurred for hundreds of years. In the nineteenth century wrestling contests took place in circuses in the USA and Europe. Later, television brought professional wrestling to a wider audience.

Gorgeous George

George Wagner transformed professional wrestling in the 1940s and 1950s and became wrestling's first TV star. He was the first to use entrance music and wear long silk robes. He even had a butler spray his opponents with perfume before they fought!

Ring rehearsals

Modern professional wrestling features paid entertainers who rehearse their wrestling moves. Most contests take place in a roped, square ring.

Throws and moves are outrageous with action often occurring outside of the ring as well.

WRESTLING FEDERATIONS

Professional wrestling is organised by different federations, including World Wrestling Entertainment (WWE). Federations sign up wrestlers and create stories and characters for them. Feuds, grudges and outrageous acts like kidnappings occur as part of the entertainment. The top wrestlers, like The Rock, Batista and The Undertaker (below), are very famous.

RING AND REAL NAMES

Hulk Hogan – Terrence Gene Bollea
The Undertaker – Mark William Calaway
Triple H – Paul Michael Levesque
Edge – Adam Joseph Copeland
The Rock – Dwayne Johnson

TOP 10 WRESTLING MOVES 4–6

Takedowns are amongst the most exciting and most important moves in wrestling. One wrestler penetrates the other wrestler's defences and uses a range of moves or throws to bring his or her opponent down onto the mat.

4 Double leg takedown

Used in freestyle and some folk wrestling, this aggressive move sees the attacker drive her shoulder low into the attacker's stomach and grip the back of her thighs. Driving her legs forward, the wrestler tilts her opponent up and back to send her onto the mat.

5 Two-on-one to single leg takedown

Used in freestyle wrestling, this starts with the attacker gripping one of her opponent's arms with both hands and pulling it down. As the opponent tries to pull up, the attacker releases the arm and locks both her hands behind the knee of one of her opponent's legs. Keeping her back straight, she can drive up, unbalance and throw her opponent.

6 Flying Mare

This is an attacking throw used in Greco-Roman wrestling. The thrower gets his own shoulder underneath his opponent's armpit and grips his upper arm. He then drops to his knees, pulling his opponent down and over his shoulder onto the mat.

WRESTLING AT THE OLYMPICS

Wrestling has been part of the modern Olympics ever since they began in 1896. Over 100 years later, wrestling is one of the most popular Olympic sports.

Olympic action

There are Olympic competitions in both freestyle and Greco-Roman wrestling. An Olympic wrestling bout consists of six minutes of action, split into three rounds of two minutes.

Medal bouts

Wrestlers in each weight division are divided into pools. The best in each pool then go into elimination bouts until the final pair of competitors compete for the gold and silver medals.

One of the most famous bouts in Olympic history occurred in 2000. After 13 remarkable years of wrestling without losing, Russian star Aleksandr Karelin (left) finally lost a bout in the final to US wrestler, Rulon Gardner.

THE LONGEST BOUT

In the early Olympics, bouts lasted until one wrestler recorded a winning move. At the 1912 Olympics, a bout between Martin Klein and Alfred Asikainen lasted for a whopping 11 hours, 40 minutes! Klein won but was too tired to compete in the final. No wonder!

Women wrestlers

It was only in 2004 that female wrestlers were admitted into the Olympics to compete in four different weight divisions in freestyle wrestling only. The gold medallists at the 2004 games were:

Weight	Gold Medallist	Country
48 kg	Irini Merleni	Ukraine
55 kg	Saori Yoshida	Japan
63 kg	Kaori Icho	Japan
72 kg	Xu Wang	China

Irini Merleni of Ukraine (red) grapples with Patricia Miranda of the USA in the semi-final of the Olympic 48 kg bout.

25

TOP 10 WRESTLING MOVES 7 — 10

Once down on the mat, both wrestlers still compete. They look for an opening or a hold or move that will win points and finish the bout. The ultimate aim is to hold an opponent's shoulders to the mat at the same time. This is a fall or pin and wins the bout.

7 Bridging

Bridging happens when a wrestler arches his or her back to keep it off the mat. Bridging is usually a defensive move to stop being pinned down, but it is also used in attack as part of the gut wrench move.

8 Gut wrench

One of the most common scoring moves on the mat, the gut wrench sees a wrestler form a strong lock of his hands around his opponent's body. He then tries to get into the bridge position and turn his opponent onto their back.

9 Half-nelson

This is a hold in which the wrestler's arm is passed under the opponent's armpit and the hand is on the back of the opponent's head. It is hard to get out of but some wrestlers manage to by turning their head away and peeling their opponent's fingers off their head.

10 Cradle move

A wrestler may be firmly on her front on the mat. One way of turning her over to pin her on her back is to use a cradle move. This sees the attacker wrap one elbow behind her opponent's knee while the other arm travels around the neck. The two hands are clasped together and then the opponent is turned.

27

FAMOUS WRESTLERS

There have been many champion wrestlers, but to be a true legend, you have to win many championships against the very best opponents.

Amazing Aleksandr

Aleksandr Karelin of Russia was considered the best Greco-Roman wrestler. Karelin was three-time Olympic champion in the heavyweight division, and remained unbeaten for a staggering 13 years before his shock loss to American Rulon Gardner.

Karelin collected nine World Championship titles and was voted the best Greco-Roman wrestler of the twentieth century.

Unbeaten legend

At the age of just 24, Osamu Watanabe's wrestling career was over. He chose to retire straight after his brilliant gold medal for Japan at the 1964 Olympics in freestyle wrestling. During all his bouts at the Olympics, he did not give away a single point.

Osamu retired with a perfect record: 186 wins and no loses.

The Canadian champ

Canada's Christine Nordhagen-Vierling won 10 Canadian and six World Championships. In 2006, she was inducted into FILA's Hall of Fame, one of the very few female wrestlers to receive this honour.

"I've cried at the worlds every single year I've won. I've always bawled. Especially when they raise that flag and the anthem is playing. You feel so proud." – Christine Nordhagen-Vierling

GLOSSARY

bout
A contest between two fighters.

breakdown
The action of getting an opponent to the mat on his or her stomach or side.

bridge
The arched position a wrestler adopts to avoid his back touching the mat.

folkstyle
A style of wrestling used in US high schools and colleges, which is similar to freestyle wrestling but with some changes to rules and added safety.

freestyle
A style of wrestling in which the legs can be targeted and also used in attacks.

Greco-Roman
A style of wrestling in which the wrestler may not attack the opponent's legs nor use his own legs to perform attacks.

penetration
The action of moving forward to penetrate an opponent's defences when attacking.

pin
Forcing both of the opponent's shoulders to the mat.

professional
Professional wrestlers earn money from fighting.

self-defence
The ability to defend yourself against attack.

singlet
The one-piece uniform worn by wrestlers.

stamina
The ability to work hard for long periods.

tactics
Different ways to fight, for example defensive tactics are used to stop an opponent's attack.

throw
Any move in which a wrestler lifts the opponent from the mat then brings him back down.

FURTHER INFORMATION

BOOKS
There are many books to read about professional wrestling, but books on sports wrestling and amateur wrestling are harder to find. If you'd like to get involved in wrestling try to find a club close to where you live.

Olympic Wrestling: Great Moments in Olympic History
Barbara M. Linde (Rosen Publishing Group, 2007)
A pictorial guide to some of the great performers and bouts in Olympic history.

Beginning Wrestling
Ryan & Sampson (Sterling Publishing, 2002)
A superb explanation of wrestling, focusing on US amateur wrestling and full of step-by-step colour photographs of key moves.

Greco-Roman Wrestling
William A. Martell (Human Kinetics, 1993)
Still widely available, this is one of the most thorough guides to Greco-Roman wrestling. Written by an Olympic coach, the book contains hundreds of black and white photographs.

Pinned
Alfred C. Martino (Harcourt Children's Books, 2005)
A novel for older children and teens about two high school wrestlers, Bobby Zane and Ivan Korske. A great read.

DVDs AND MOVIES

Throws and Takedowns: Freestyle Wrestling Basic / Intermediate, 2005.
Two great instructional DVDs from Geoff Thompson and available from Summersdale Productions.

Some of these movies are not suitable for viewers of all ages.

Vision Quest (1985)
A quality 'feelgood' movie all about a high school wrestler, Louden Swain, played by Matthew Modine.

Reversal (2001)
Packed with realistic wrestling scenes, this film features Danny Mousetis as a wrestler struggling with the demands of training and coaching from his father.

WEBSITES
http://www.fila-wrestling.com/
The official website of FILA, the organisation that runs world wrestling. It features lots of news and competition results, coach's corner and much more.

http://www.britishwrestling.org/
The home on the internet of the British Wrestling Association.

http://www.usawrestling.org/
The official website of USA Wrestling with results, national rankings, competitions and a huge database of wrestling clubs, searchable by state.

INDEX

Asikainen, Alfred 25

Bobis, Gyula 13
bridging 26, 30

Commonwealth Games 19
cradle, the 27
Cross, Kendal 18
Cruise, Tom 4
Cumberland and Westmoreland
   wrestling 10

divisions, weight 13, 24, 25

equipment 14, 15
European Wrestling
   Championships 12
Evala 9

federations 21
FILA 29, 31
films 4, 31
   Reversal 31
   The World According to Garp 4
   Vision Quest 31

folkstyle wrestling 11, 30
folk wrestling 10-11, 22, 30
freestyle wrestling 11, 12, 13, 19,
   22, 24, 25, 29, 30

Gardner, Rulon 24, 28
Glima 10
Greco-Roman wrestling 7, 12,
   13, 23, 24, 28, 30, 31
Greece, ancient 7

Gruenwald, Jim 18
gut wrench, the 26

half-nelson, the 27
headlock, the 16, 17
history (of wrestling) 6-7

Irving, John 4

Jiao li 6
Jordanov, Valentin 19

Karelin, Aleksandr 24, 28
Kim, Min-chul 5
Kim, Young-nam 14
Klein, Martin 25
Kroton, Milo of 7

Lincoln, Abraham 4

Merleni, Irini 25
Miranda, Patricia 25
Mohammed, Ghulum 6
moves, wrestling 16-17, 22-23,
   26-27
movies (see films)

Nordhagen-Vierling,
   Christine 29

Olympics 7, 13, 14, 15, 18,
   24-25, 28, 29, 31

Pehlwani 6
professionals 9, 20-21

rules 5, 8-9, 10-11, 13, 16,
   24, 26, 30
Ruzikulov, Rawshan 5

Sambo 9
Schwingen 8
Sumo 9

takedowns 16, 17, 22, 23
television 20-21
tie-ups 16-17
training 14-15, 18-19

underhook, the 17
Uyoalah, Nick 19

Vikings 10

Wagner, George 20
Washington, George 4, 5
Watanabe, Osamu 29
Williams, Robin 4
women wrestlers 15, 25, 29
World Championships 28, 29
World Wrestling Entertainment
   21

Yagli Güres 11

Zummo, Vickie 15